D0487834

# Make Hay While the Sun Shines

## A Book of Proverbs

# Make Hay
# While the Sun Shines

A Book of Proverbs
chosen by Alison M. Abel

*illustrated by Shirley Hughes*

*faber and faber*

First published in 1977
This edition first published in 1998
by Faber and Faber Limited
3 Queen Square London WC1N 3AU

Typeset by Faber and Faber Ltd
Printed in England by Clays Ltd, St Ives plc

A CIP record for this book
is available from the British Library

ISBN 0–571–19439–7

2 4 6 8 10 9 7 5 3 1

# Introduction

Proverbs have enriched our everyday language for centuries. Like fables, they often contain a strong warning or moral and take us back to lost rural skills. Many derive from the Bible. But the imagery is wonderfully lively and full of comic absurdities. It comes up as fresh as a daisy to any listening child, whatever their ethnic background, who puzzles to make sense of it.

Discontented leopards, counterfeit gold, cats and kings may be the stuff of fairy tales. But uncertainly tempered sleeping dogs, predatory early birds and overenthusiastic cooks are still very much with us. The fun of putting the literal image alongside a simple explanation is irresistible.

*Shirley Hughes*

# Contents

Make hay while the sun shines

*Do a job when the time seems right. (If you leave it you may not get such a good opportunity again.)*

Look before you leap

*Be sure you know what you're letting yourself in for before you do anything drastic*

All work and no play makes Jack a dull boy

*You won't do your work well if you don't rest and play too*

A stitch in time saves nine

*If you put something right as soon as it goes wrong,
you won't have so much trouble later*

Many hands make light work

*A job is done more quickly and easily if a lot of people help*

Too many cooks spoil the broth

*If too many people all try to do the same work at the same time, they can make a dreadful mess of it!*

Every cloud has a silver lining

*Even the worst things that happen have a good side to them*

Don't count your chickens before they're hatched

*Don't plan too far ahead, and don't rely on things
always turning out well for you*

The early bird catches the worm

*If you want the best, then you must get there first –*
*late-comers miss their chance*

A bird in the hand is worth two in the bush

*What you have is worth more to you than something twice as valuable that you haven't got*

People who live in glass houses shouldn't throw stones

*Don't criticize other people if you have the same faults yourself*

The leopard can't change his spots

*People can't change the way they are made*

Let sleeping dogs lie

*Don't stir up trouble*

Once bitten, twice shy

*People who have been upset or hurt once don't risk the same thing happening again*

It's no use crying over spilt milk

*Once you've made a mistake, worrying about it won't put things right*

# A watched pot never boils

*Things you are waiting for seem never to happen if you keep thinking about them. (Forget them, and you may be taken by surprise!)*

The grass is always greener on the other side

*What you haven't got always looks better than what you have*

The night is always darkest just before the dawn

*Things are always at their worst just before they start to get better*

Great oaks from little acorns grow

*Important things often start in a small way*

It's no use keeping a dog and barking yourself

*If you ask other people to do something for you, let them get on with it and don't try to take over*

All that glitters is not gold

*Not everything that looks attractive is really valuable*

29

Don't put all your eggs in one basket

*Don't rely too much on one particular thing. (Then you won't lose everything if you are let down.)*

Don't have too many irons in the fire

*Don't try to do too many things at the same time*

A cat may look at a king

*We all have a right to our own opinions, even about the most important people*

Pride goes before a fall

*Self-important people come to grief sooner or later*

Don't change horses in mid-stream

*If you've started doing something one way, don't change your methods half-way through*

If you've made your bed you must lie on it

*If you've made a mistake you must put up with the results*

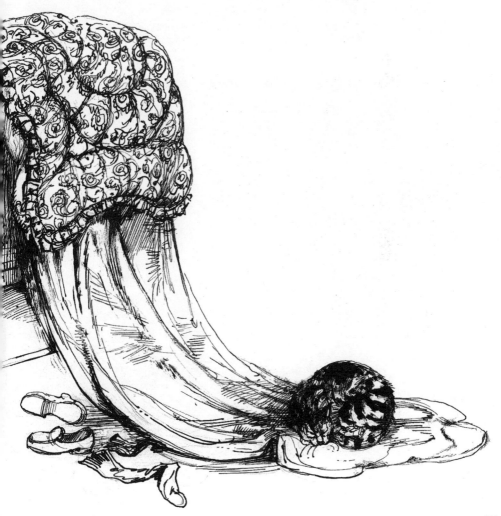

Jack of all trades is master of none

*Someone who does a lot of different things is unlikely to do any of them very well*

While the cat's away the mice will play

*People do as they please when the person
they are afraid of is out of the way*

40